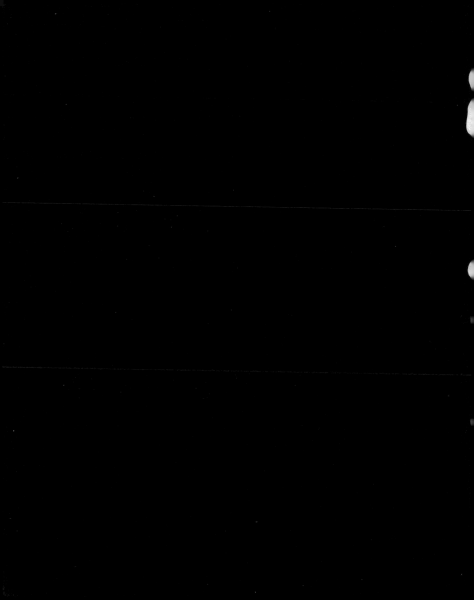

JOSEPH'S BONES

a collection of stories

written and illustrated by

OZZIE NOGG

*For Carol —
with love
from Ozzie
October 2004*

OZNAS
BOOKS

ISBN: 0-9753988-0-6

Library of Congress Control Number

2004093981

The author wishes to acknowledge the generous
support of The Jewish Heritage Preservation Project

Book design by Patty O'Connor-Seger
NewIDEAS, Starkville, MS

Published in the United States of America
by
OZNAS BOOKS
P.O. Box 3353
Omaha, NE 68103-0353

אהבה

Dear Donald,

*Before anything else is said,
know that this comes to you
with love and gratitude
from the rabbi's daughter.*

Contents

Joseph's Bones:
An Explanation, A Dedication

One Friday night in the winter of 2004, our granddaughter, Alexandra (aged six at the time), slept over at our apartment. During the course of her visit I mislaid my favorite pair of earrings, but the lost were soon found, to my delight and to Alex's as well.

"Oh, Bubbie," she said, "I'm *soooo* glad you found the earrings because when you die and we get your jewelry, those earrings are what I was going to pick."

Bless her heart. As soon as the words left her lips, she tried to dig herself out of the hole she'd dug herself (and me) into. She looked so adorable in her distress, I wanted to give her the earrings right then, but they seemed a paltry inheritance.

Alex's words, of course, stayed with me, forcing me to consider (yet again) my mortality. To consider what legacy I might leave my children and grandchildren. A legacy that would not be consigned to attic or cellar, but remain upon their hearts, to be spoken of in their homes and carried with them on their way. And so we have this collection of personal family stories. But why the title, *Joseph's Bones*? Read on . . .

According to the book of Genesis, there came a time when Jacob received word that his son, Joseph, was alive and ruling over the whole of Egypt. Then Jacob and his entire family came down from Canaan to live in Egypt, and Joseph treated his father and brothers with love and generosity.

For seventeen years, Jacob lived with Joseph in great happiness. And when Jacob's end was near, he blessed his sons and said, *Soon I will be gathered to my fathers. Take me up from this strange place and bury me in the land of Canaan in the cave of Machpelah alongside Abraham and*

Sarah, Isaac and Rebecca, and Leah. And Joseph replied, *I will do as you ask.* Then Jacob breathed his last and was gathered to his people, and Joseph and his brothers took their father up to Canaan and buried him with his ancestors.

The family saga continues.

Joseph and his brothers returned to Egypt where Joseph lived to see the third generation of his children's children. And when he was one hundred and ten years old, Joseph said to his brothers, *I am about to die. But God will surely remember you, and take you up out of this land to the land he promised to Abraham, Isaac and Jacob.* And Joseph made his brothers swear that when God redeemed the Hebrews and returned them to the Promised Land, his bones would not be left behind. On his deathbed, Joseph made his family swear, saying, *God will surely remember you, and then you shall carry up my bones from here with you.* Then Joseph died and was placed in a coffin in Egypt.

Legend has it that Joseph's bones lay in that coffin during more than four hundred years of Egyptian slavery, until the night of the Exodus. In their frantic dash to freedom, the Children of Israel hastily strapped on their sandals and stuffed provisions into sacks. But Moses (more loyal to the past than to possessions, and determined to honor the promise given to his ancestor centuries earlier) took precious time to search for Joseph's coffin. After all, he reasoned, commitments to others aren't cancelled by the grave. But how, after all these years, could Moses find where Joseph was buried?

Enter Serah bat Asher, who, it is said, came down from Canaan to Egypt with Jacob, her grandfather. On the eve of the Exodus, Serah was an old, wise woman – a teller of stories, a keeper of memories. Immortal, a survivor, she alone had spanned the generations from Joseph to Moses. She alone held the secret of where Joseph's bones were buried.

Moses, my master, she whispered. *Joseph's*

iron casket lies sunk in the depths of the Nile, hidden there by Egyptian wizards. And Moses stood at the river's edge and called, *Joseph, Joseph, the hour of redemption has come.* The waters belched and bubbled, and when the coffin bobbed to the surface, we are told that Moses seized it, in joy, and took the bones of Joseph with him.

During the forty years of wandering in the desert, the story continues. It tells of the two arks that the Children of Israel carried with them. One ark contained the Ten Commandments – the words that teach us how to live – and the other contained Joseph's bones – the remains of an ancestor long dead. And for all the years it took our people to come back home, the bones were carefully guarded and treated with respect. And before Moses died, he handed them to Joshua. And Joseph's bones, which the Israelites had brought up from Egypt, were buried at Shechem in the piece of land that Jacob bought for a hundred pieces of silver from the sons of Hamor, the father of Shechem. And this became the inheritance of Joseph's descendants.

So there you have it.

Joseph's Bones.

A symbol of continuity, memory, and promises kept. A metaphor linking one generation to another. That's the reason for the title. And for this dedication.

To
Kathy, Larry, Zachary and Seth
Marsha and Shari
Shelly, Mike, Alexandra and Natalie
Tony, Patty and Olivia

Wherever you go,
take my stories, like Joseph's bones,
and carry them with you

BUBBIE'S HOUSE

FOR THE FIRST FEW years of my life we lived with my mother's mother, my Bubbie, Rochel. That was her Yiddish name, Rochel. Here in America she was called Rose.

My Bubbie's house was small, simple, painted white. It stood high on the 7th Street hill in Duluth. In the winter, if I squinched my eyes tight, the house and the snow and the sky all blended together, and the angels I made in the snow spun straight up to heaven.

In the summer the front yard was thick with clover and orange butterflies, and when I lay down in the yard I could roll over and over, down, down, faster and faster, straight down into Bubbie's garden — her garden of tiny sweet peas, and of carrots we ate still warm from the earth. Her garden with stalks of dill, like green lace, and cucumbers small as my thumb.

On the front of my Bubbie's house was a porch. The floor was painted a shiny dark gray, and a swing hung down from the ceiling on two chains. In the cool Duluth evenings, I'd sit on that swing with my Bubbie while she told me stories about her life in the old country.

In my village, the snow fell so fast and piled up so high, it covered the rooftops...

My momma dug holes in the dirt floor of our house — a dirt floor, just imagine — and in those holes she stored potatoes and onions and beets because who knew from an icebox...

I never, ever, ever had to go to school because

I was a girl...

My Bubbie told wonderful stories.

The kitchen in Bubbie's house was my favorite room. Black iron pots of spinach borscht, potato dumplings, and *p'cha* simmered on the stove, and wondrous food baked in the oven. Stuffed cabbage. Apricot strudel. A cow's tongue. One day I peeked inside the oven and a whole fish — its grinning mouth full of sharp little teeth, its eyes open — stared back at me. And because of the cooking, the kitchen windows were always covered with steam. Once, my Bubbie wrote my name with her finger in the steam on the window, and then she held me while we both watched the steam vanish and take my name with it. But then Bubbie showed me that if I breathed on the window — *whoooooo* — my name would come back, like magic.

My Bubbie died before any of my children got to know her very well, but I told them all her stories. I told them about her house.

And then one summer, I decided it was time we took a trip to Duluth. It would be nice, I said, to spend some time with my old Uncle Harry who still lived there. But my real reason for going back was to show my kids my Bubbie's house. And when we drove up the hill to 7th Street, there it was, exactly as I remembered it. The porch. The swing. The clover. Even the butterflies.

I wanted to ring the bell and introduce myself to the people who lived there. *May I please come inside? I need to go into the kitchen and breathe on the window and see if my name will come back.* But I was afraid the people might think I was crazy, so I sat in the swing on the porch and watched the snow fall on my Bubbie's village, watched it cover the rooftops while my husband and kids stood in the yard, butterflies swarming around their legs.

Later that day I told my Uncle Harry what we had done. "Uncle Harry," I said. "Today we took the kids to see Bubbie's house on 7th Street."

And my sweet Uncle Harry put his thin, old arms around me and whispered, "*Oi*, Osnehleh. Osnehleh. Bubbie's house was on 8th Street. And they tore it down years ago."

Maybe the old saying is true. God gave us memory so we could have roses in the wintertime.

ONE LITTLE KID

EVERY YEAR, RIGHT after Purim, my Bubbie painted her pantry. Every single year. Eventually the layers of white paint got so thick that the cupboard doors wouldn't close all the way, and the paint never quite dried. If you pressed your fingernail into it months later, at Rosh Hashanah, perhaps, you'd still make a small curved impression. It was faint, but you could see it. This always filled me with wonder.

Into that magical pantry went the Pesach dishes, clear and green and fragile. My Bubbie let me help her stack them on the shelves. I was little, but she trusted me. Things like that you don't forget.

I remember Momma and Bubbie, both with their hair coiled in tight buns, cleaning the house before Pesach. They scoured every surface in the kitchen, dumped *chometz* crumbs from drawers, shook them from apron pockets and beat them out of rugs. They carried pots and pans in bushel baskets down to the basement, carried other pots and pans in bushel baskets up from the basement. And all the time, they laughed. While polishing silver, ironing curtains, chopping fish. To me, preparing for Pesach looked like forced labor in a house of bondage, but to my mother and grandmother it was joy.

I also remember searching for *chometz* on the night before the Seder. In our shadowy, almost-dark house, my brother and I put ten pieces of bread on the window sills and then, by the light of a candle, we led our parents to the leaven. Solemnly, using a feather, Poppa swept the crumbs onto a wooden spoon. Then Momma wrapped everything up in a cloth and put the bundle outside for the night. In the morning, with much ceremony and many benedictions, we burned the *chometz* to ashes. As we watched the gray, feathery pieces drift away, Poppa said, "When the *chometz* goes up in smoke, so do our evil inclinations." I didn't understand what he meant at the time, but I remember his words.

Setting the Seder table in my childhood home was serious business, with specific rituals and rules. Elijah's heavy silver kiddush cup stood beside Bubbie's brass candlesticks. *(I carried these on the boat, wrapped in my shawl, all the way to America.)* Plates were strategically arranged on the lace cloth so as to cover up the indelible wine stains from past Seders. A chipped goblet? Give it to Aunt Fanny or Uncle Sam, not to a guest! My special Seder responsibility was to make the salt water for the eggs, and the gravity of the assignment was not lost on me. I measured and mixed and trembled, and when Momma gave the water her taste-test, she always, *always* said it was perfect. In that moment, a tiny undiscovered bit of *chometz* in me swelled with pride.

Poppa opens the Haggadah. *This is the bread of affliction*, the story begins. Four questions. Four children. (*Please let me be the smart one!*) Poppa turns pages, does not skip a word. Bored, my thoughts wandering with the Arameans, I slide from my chair down under the tablecloth, in my tent, encamped by the sea, until a mighty hand and outstretched arm pulls me from the sand to count frogs, boils, locusts in drops of wine, a circle, perfect, complete.

Even a Peretz, a Sholem Aleichem, would

lack words to describe our Seder meal. Poppa's five-alarm-grated-by-hand horseradish. Chicken soup (*see how the circles of fat swim like gold coins*), tiny unborn eggs and matzoh balls fluffy as pillows. Crunchy potato pudding crowned with fried onions and *gribenehs*. Chopped liver, mounds of young green asparagus, bottomless bowls of sweet sticky *tzimmis, gedempteh* chicken awash in gravy, brisket with prunes, strawberry ices, macaroons, sponge cake rising tall as the Tower of Babel, *Dayenu!* Oh, how I pitied the hungry, wandering Hebrews who had to settle for manna from heaven.

The food that took days to prepare is gone in minutes, the dishes back in the kitchen. My spoiled cousin, Leon, finds the *afikomen* (*he's bigger, it's not fair*) and we begin again.

Friends, let us give thanks. Bless Poppa, my teacher. Bless Momma, my teacher. Bless all of us, me and my family together and all that is ours.

Now turn off the lights for Elijah the Prophet *(the wine in his cup — look — it moved!)* sing Hallel new stains on the tablecloth dizzy with wine half asleep I am one Adir Hu knows two zuzim Chad Gadya cat dog stick fire water ox shochet *(ooooo here it comes…)* Angel *(stop!)* Death *(sha I'm holding you)* wrapped in her arms safe where nothing can get me next year *(sleep my mammeleh sleep)* there in Bubbie's lap *(sleep now)* the Seder is over, a circle, complete. Once more the Hebrew children escape the Angel of Death. And so do I.

Every year, right after Purim, she painted her pantry. Every single year. Now I am the Bubbie who creates memories and holds them tight. The role suits me.

But at Pesach, quite frankly, I'd much rather still be the kid.

AARON'S AGGIE

WHEN I WAS A LITTLE girl growing up, I was a real tomboy. Even had my very own pocket knife that I won off of Benji Goldfarb when I beat him at arm wrestling. Two out of three.

So, anyway. When I was growing up I lived right down the block from my cousin, Aaron. Aaron is four years older than I am and back then, when I was eight and Aaron was twelve, he was my hero, even bigger than Captain Marvel. You see, my cousin Aaron was the undisputed marble

13

champion of Jefferson Grade School. There wasn't a kid for miles around who could come even close to beating him. It was like Aaron's marbles were magic, especially his shooter. It was a bright green aggie shooter and it never missed. Sometimes I thought that aggie was alive and could actually see where it was going.

Now, being the marble champion meant my cousin Aaron was really, really, *really* popular. All the kids at school thought he was so swell. Even the guys he *beat* wanted to be his friends. And so I started thinking that if I had my cousin Aaron's marbles, especially his shooter, that would be even better than having Benji Goldfarb's pocket knife.

So one day after school I'm watching my cousin Aaron beat the pants off some guys for about the umpteenth time and I say to him, "Hey, Aaron, how about I swap you my pocket knife for your shooter."

And Aaron looks at me and says, "How many times do I have to tell you? Girls don't play with pocket knives. Or marbles. Girls play jump rope and jacks and dolls. Now beat it." Sometimes Aaron acted like such a big shot, what with him being four years older than me and the marble champion to boot. And it's then I start thinking of ways to get my hands on that shooter. I try *not* to think it, but I can't stop. I'm wondering if maybe my cousin Aaron is even *worse* at arm wrestling than Benji Goldfarb.

So, here's what happens next.

One really, really, *really* cold winter day at recess a new kid challenges my cousin Aaron to a game. The poor kid. Being new and all, he doesn't know that right from the start he's a dead duck. So, my cousin Aaron and the new kid, they get down on their hands and knees in the snow and ice and scratch out a circle. And the rest of us are watching and jumping around to keep warm and my cousin Aaron and the new kid keep blowing on their hands — their fingers are freezing — and then Aaron gets ready to shoot.

First he shuts his left eye real tight like he always does. Then he opens up his aiming eye real wide and stares down his thumb like he always does. Then he lines up the green aggie shooter, real careful, like he always does and then *Zap! Kapowee!* Rainbows and immies fly all over the schoolyard and my cousin Aaron wins again like he always does. Then he takes this special rag out of his coat pocket and wipes all the snow and gravel and gunk off the marbles and then he polishes his shooter and polishes it and polishes it until I swear, that green aggie is winking at me.

Well, next thing you know, my cousin Aaron, probably from sitting around in the snow that day playing marbles, he comes down with this bad cold. And while he's stuck at home in bed eating chicken soup, I try *not* to but I can't help thinking this cold could make Aaron really, really, *really* weak, so maybe now is the perfect time to arm wrestle him for that shooter. And then things take an unexpected turn.

What happens is, my cousin Aaron's cold gets worse and he winds up in St. Ignatius Hospital with nurses in nun's outfits. And Bubbie says, "Go tell me somebody how a nice Jewish boy will get better in a place with *traif* food in a room with a cross *p'tui p'tui* over his bed."

Now, I don't know if it's the *traif* or the cross or what, but Aaron doesn't get better. And then Momma tells me that somehow the cold has traveled around Aaron's body and settled in his eye.

"A cold can travel?"

"Go ask the smart doctors," Momma says, "all day going in and out of Aaron's room, examining him and whispering and scratching their heads, the smart doctors from fancy schools who should know how to make the child better."

Well finally, *finally* the doctors figure out what to do and they take my cousin Aaron and *Zap! Kapowee!* they cut his eye right out of his head. And it's his aiming eye, at that.

I cannot believe it. "Momma, are you *sure*? Are you sure they cut his eye right out of his head?"

"I'm sure. But it could be worse. He could, God forbid, be blind."

And I'm saying to myself, *Without his aiming eye he might as well be.*

And I try not to but I can't help thinking, *Whoa. Without his aiming eye, my cousin Aaron probably won't need that green aggie shooter ever again.*

Well, finally my cousin Aaron comes home from the hospital and I go visit him and he's lying on the davenport in the front room in his bathrobe and he's got this black patch over the place where his aiming eye used to be. He looks like a pirate.

"Hey. You look like a pirate," I say.

"No kidding," my cousin Aaron says.

"Yeah. No kidding."

So I'm sitting here, and my cousin Aaron is

lying there, and it's really, really, *really* quiet. And finally my cousin Aaron says, "While I was in the hospital I learned how to play chess. The guy in the next bed taught me."

And I say, "No kidding."

"Yeah. No kidding."

And then my cousin Aaron says, "You may not know this, but it takes brains to play chess. It's a very difficult game. You gotta be really, really, *really* smart to play chess. And grown up, too. It's not like marbles, which is only for stupid babies."

And I'm thinking, *For babies! That's me! This is my chance. And I won't even have to arm wrestle him for it.*

So I say, "Well, as long as you're too grown up to play marbles anymore, can I have your shooter? I mean, if you're only going to play chess, you don't need the thing any more, right?"

And my cousin Aaron stares at me and stares at me and I can tell he's thinking about it and I'm praying *please please please oh please Aaron pleeeese* and finally, *finally* my cousin Aaron yanks that black patch off and *Zap! Kapowee!* He still has two eyes but one of them, *honest*, is bright green and it's winking at me.

THE CAP POPPA GOT FROM THE CZAR

I CAN'T REMEMBER A Hanukkah without snow. Snow in drifts as tall as a man. And that man? My Poppa-the-Rabbi, trudging home from shul in the evening darkness to light the candles. Poppa with a wool muffler over his nose, rubber galoshes flopping on his feet, and his head warmed by a Persian lamb fur cap.

On any given Hanukkah night, Poppa would stomp into the house, blow the snowflakes

21

off the cap and say, "So, did I ever tell you who gave me this cap?" He'd asked this question many times before, and of course I knew the answer. But pretending I didn't was part of our family's Hanukkah tradition.

"No, Poppa. Who gave you the cap?"

"The cap? The cap was given to me by Czar Nicholas, himself."

"Really, Poppa! When?"

"When I was seven, maybe eight. It was Hanukkah and Czar Nicholas just happened to be passing by our village when, through the open window, he heard me singing *Maoz tzuuuur y'shoo-a-seeeee*. He was very impressed."

"What did Czar Nicholas do then, Poppa?"

"What did he do then? He walked straight into our house, put the cap on my head, shook my hand and said, 'You may call me Nikki'."

And from the kitchen Mama would yell, "*Oi*, Alex! Such stories you tell her."

The Hanukkah candles we lit when I was a child were fat, sturdy and o r a n g e. Not plain-Jane orange, mind you, but *orange*. And when those candles stood in the frosty window, their flames melting the ice until it puddled on the sill, well...anyone passing by knew he was looking at candles that meant business. *Don't mess with us*, they seemed to say, *if you know what's good for you*. Just like the Maccabees.

While the candles burned on those long-ago evenings, I spun my *dreidel* and Poppa sang his Hanukkah songs, in Hebrew, Yiddish, Russian, English. I loved the singing, really I did, but Momma wouldn't start frying her *latkes* until the singing was over and the candles burned down to nubs, and sitting through Poppa's Hanukkah concerts in anticipation of those *latkes* wasn't easy. Mama's *latkes*, you see, were the true miracle of Hanukkah.

"And what makes the taste of Momma's *latkes* so miraculous?" Poppa asked every year.

And every year my response was the same. "The secret ingredient!"

"And what is the secret ingredient?"

I knew the answer, but pretending I didn't was part of the tradition. "Tell me, Poppa! What is the secret ingredient?"

Then Poppa would put down his fork, wipe the sour cream off his moustache, take Momma's hand and whisper, "The secret ingredient is the tiny piece of her knuckle she grates in along with the potatoes."

Blushing, Momma would say, "*Oi*, Alex. Such stories you tell her."

Growing up, I knew nothing about Hanukkah shopping lists or fancy wrapping and bows. And a gift every night? Never. I got one present and one present only. Hanukkah *gelt* that Poppa took from his trouser pocket and put, unwrapped, in my palm. Every Hanukkah the gift was the same. An uncirculated 1923 silver dollar that Poppa had somehow gotten his hands on the year he came to America. He kept a stash of these coins in a black wool sock hidden behind our stove. I don't know who he thought he was hiding them from. I knew where the treasure was. And Poppa knew that I knew. But pretending I didn't know was also part of our family's Hanukkah tradition. And we observed that tradition until the fateful Hanukkah of 1944.

It was the day of the fifth candle. We woke to find the radio… gone! The Victrola… gone! In the kitchen, Poppa moved the stove. *Oi, vey! Gevalt! Ganeyvim!* Unlike the small jar of oil that kept burning in the Hanukkah story, our seemingly inexhaustible treasure had vanished. Stolen while we slept by some non-sectarian Grinch.

I wept. Poppa fumed. Then he put on his coat and fur cap and marched straight to the bank. That night, as he had done for years, Poppa gave me my Hanukkah *gelt*. I turned the coin over and over, studied its face. It was familiar but somehow different. And then I realized what was wrong. The dollar wasn't engraved *1-9-2-3*. The numbers on this silver dollar were *1-9-4-4*.

"Poppa?"

"*Tochter.* See how it shines, so bright, so new. This new gift is much better than the old."

And Momma sighed, "*Oi*, Alex. Such stories you tell her."

Looking back, I realize that a child more perceptive than I would have gotten a clue, right then, that more than just dates on silver dollars can change. Now, when I gather with my children and grandchildren to celebrate the Festival of Lights, it's good, of course. But my Hanukkah is gone. It's been replaced by frantic shopping and a gift every night and candles that are thin, pale imitations of the real thing. Sadly, the *latkes* are often made from a mix. The snowdrifts are seldom tall as a man. And the singing rarely merits a reward from the Czar.

It's then I run back to a magical time. I taste my mother's *latkes*, hear my father's Hanukkah songs. I remember his stories and feel the silver coins in my hand. These riches can never be stolen. They are secure, safe — along with the knowledge that hidden deep in the bottom of my dresser is the cap Poppa got from the Czar.

MY BROTHER'S KEEPER

ON THE NIGHT IT ALL happened, I was eleven, my brother Michael was four, and we lived with Momma and Poppa in a house on a corner, on a bus stop.

Living on a bus stop may seem like no big deal, like something not worth mentioning. But to us it was really important because we didn't have a car, so if we wanted to go anywhere we had to take the bus. Of course, we never went anywhere except to *shul* and we always walked to *shul*, but the bus is really important to this story. You'll see.

I have to stop here and tell you that today, my brother Michael is tall and muscled and very good looking. He's also remarkably well adjusted. I mention this because on the night we almost but not quite became orphans, four-year-old Michael was fat and cross-eyed and saw monsters in every corner and still sucked his thumb. Plus, he lisped. But to his credit, Michael worshipped and adored me, qualities I found particularly endearing and used to my advantage whenever I could.

Now, you should also know that my parents, the rabbi and *rebbitzen*, were not social butterflies, and were content to spend all their evenings at home with just Michael and me for company. Poppa listened to Yiddish records on the Victrola. Sometimes he studied a sacred text. Momma embroidered dishtowels and tablecloths and pillowcases in perfect cross-stitch with tiny French knots. And every night of his four years, my brother Michael took comfort and refuge in this constant togetherness.

I, on the other hand — eleven years old and on the cusp of womanhood — fantasized my escape from this smothering cocoon. And on the night we almost but not quite became orphans, I almost but not quite got my wish.

What happened was this.

It was a dreary January afternoon, only four-thirty but already dark. The snow had been falling for days. We'd just finished an early supper and I was helping Momma dry the dishes when she announced, "Tonight we are going to the movies."

"The movies, the *mooovies*!" I chirped. "Which movie are we going to, Momma?"

And Momma answered, "Not *we*, as in all of us. *We*, as in Poppa and me. *We* are going to the movies. *You* are staying home with your brother. You're old enough now to take care of him for a few hours."

I was crushed and deeply disappointed, but Momma had recognized my maturity, and in that moment I grew six inches and sprouted breasts. Michael sat dumbstruck, tears welling up in his little crossed eyes.

"We'll catch the five o'clock bus," Momma said. "The movie starts at five-thirty. It ends at seven. We'll be home by seven-thirty. Seven-thirty on the dot." Michael grabbed the hem of my skirt.

"From the window you can see the bus stop," Poppa reminded us. "And you know the bus. It's always on time."

Then Momma and Poppa pulled on their galoshes, buttoned their coats, wrapped mufflers around their necks, put on hats and mittens, kissed us and — for the first time ever — walked out the door and left us behind. Just like that.

I ran to the window, dragging Michael, still plastered like a barnacle to my skirt. We pressed our faces to the frosty glass and we could see them. At the bus stop, in the eerie glow from the street light, Momma and Poppa shimmered like ghosts. And then at five o'clock, right on time, the bus pulled up, our parents got on and with a casual wave, vanished into the night.

Michael clung to my legs. "I'm thcared, Othie. It'th thho... dark."

"Oh, you are such a baby," I said, grandly. But to calm his childish fears I marched from room to room — Michael at my heels — and turned on every lamp and light in the house, including the one over the bathtub and the small, naked bulbs in the closets.

Back in the living room it was very quiet. All I heard was the snow, creaking on the roof, Michael's soft sniffling and the tick of the mantle clock which, by now, read *six*.

Michael stood at the window, twisting his hair, sucking his thumb. "Will it be theven-thirty thoon, Othie?"

"Don't be silly. It won't be seven-thirty for hours and hours...and hours." I lounged on the sofa reading *Little Women*, overcome with pity for poor, sick Beth.

"Can a buth get thtuck in the thno, Othie?"

"Oh, sure. You bet. Every winter dozens and dozens of buses get stuck in the snow and they have to sit there for months and months and months until the snow melts in the spring. Now get away from the window, Michael, and put on your pajamas."

Michael didn't move but the hands on the clock did. *Six-fifteen. Six-thirty. Seven.* Michael's sniffling grew to sobs. He stood at the window, rigid as Lot's wife. I got up from the sofa, dragged him to his room and dumped him on the bed.

"What if Momma and Poppa get lotht in the thno, Othie?"

I yanked off his shoes and socks.

"Oh, Othie, what if the buth and Momma

and Poppa get lotht in the thno and never come back…?"

I peeled off his overalls, pulled the undershirt over his head, stuffed him into his Doctor Dentons and grabbed him tight by the shoulders. "Michael. If Momma and Poppa get lost in the snow and never come back, we…will…be… *orphans.*"

He stared at me, open mouthed, mute.

"Yes, Michael. We will be *orphans.* And I will have to take care of you. And you will have to obey me and do everything I tell you to do because I am bigger than you are, Michael. Much, much bigger. That's what will happen if Momma and Poppa get lost in the snow and never… come … back …!"

With that, he crawled under the covers and curled up into a shivering, hiccuping ball.

"One of these days, Michael," I said as I swept out of his room, "one of these days you are going to *thmother* to death under there."

In the front room, the hands on the clock

pointed to seven-thirty. Seven-thirty on the dot. *Little Women* lay abandoned on the sofa. I took up Michael's place at the window and stared into the night. Nothing moved in the street. No cars. No people. No bus. The falling snowflakes were big as goose feathers, the drifts tall as mountains, and by seven forty-five I had shrunk back to my original height.

By eight o'clock I was once again flat chested as a boy.

By eight-fifteen I was crying in earnest. Through the blur I saw the headline:

EXTRA! EXTRA! Rabbi and Wife Found Frozen in Stuck Bus! The sub-head read: *Orphaned Daughter Vows To Care For Baby Brother.*

At eight-thirty, all hope gone, I began to weep for my poor, dead parents, frozen stiff and blue, buried in the drifts.

At nine o'clock I moaned and beat my breast and repented my cruelty toward poor, innocent

Michael. Michael, who trusted me and loved me and with whom I was now doomed to spend the rest of my days.

At nine-thirty I cried for myself and for all the lost possibilities. The gay romances, the heady adventures, the fame and fortune I would never know because I would, instead, be teaching Michael to tie his shoes or driving him to the speech therapist.

Finally, at ten o'clock, spent of tears, resigned to my fate, I sank to the floor in a swoon like Beth March, my young life nipped in the bud.

And then, at some point during the night we almost but not quite became orphans, there stood Poppa carrying Michael, limp and damp, his soft, bubbly snores the only signs of life.

"Such good care you took of your brother," Poppa whispered. "Look how he sleeps, like an angel."

And then I was in Momma's lap, my face buried in the fur collar of her coat while she rocked me in her arms and crooned, "*Oi*, Osneleh, Osneleh, the bus got stuck in the snow. We never meant to leave you alone for so long. I'm sorry, Osneleh. I'm so, so sorry. *Sha. Sha*. We're home. Don't cry, we're home."

And I said, "No, Momma, I'm crying because of *Little Women*. I'm crying because Beth died."

And my wise Momma kissed my wet, swollen eyes and said, "Of course. I understand. Even stories people make up can seem just like real."

A LESSON IN THE WATERMELON

UNMET EXPECTATIONS make me nuts. I trace this back to the watershed night in 1940 when I did not win the Shirley Temple look-alike contest on which my entire family thought I had a lock. In spite of my blond curls and the ability to sing *On the Good Ship Lollipop* like an angel, I received second prize and my first lesson in dealing with dashed dreams. This lesson was repeated a few years later when I tap-danced my little toes off in a Major Bowes Talent Contest, only to be out-applause-metered by a kid who played *Amapola*, flat, on the accordion. He won the trip to Hollywood and the screen test I'd been counting on. Talk about shock and surprise. Talk about wounded pride. A quart of cod-liver oil would have been easier to swallow.

I tried to be a better sport. I did my best to be gracious in defeat, to mumble *Cngrtlashns*, and shake the winner's hand without crushing the bones. But on the infamous day when my best friend (she, who shall remain nameless) beat me out as 4th Grade Talmud Torah Purim Queen (an honor for which I considered myself a shoo-in), there was no end to my despair. I wailed against the injustice (like Esau, I'd been robbed of my birthright) but by then it was clear. Life doesn't always go as planned. Even now, when things don't turn out the way I expect them to or think they should, I hear my little kid voice whining, "That is *not* the way it was supposed to happen." And then I think of my father.

Poppa came to America from Lithuania in 1923. He arrived with a forged passport, his rabbinic ordination and the ability to wake up every morning, thank God that he was still breathing and get on with his life. He lived ninety-three years and believe me, many of his expectations were not fulfilled. But when things didn't turn out the way he anticipated, I never heard him say, "That is *not* the way it was supposed to happen." Nope. When Poppa ran into one of life's unexpected detours he simply shook his head, sighed, and said, in Yiddish, *Dos hoben mir nisht g'ler'nt in cheder*. This we never learned in school.

He said it when not one of my three brothers chose to become a rabbi.

He said it when my mother died, suddenly and much too young.

He said it when several of his grandchildren married outside the faith.

Dos hoben mir nisht g'ler'nt in cheder.

Unlike me, Poppa had a healthy attitude when it came to expectations that don't pan out. Like the time he planted watermelon.

It was spring, a few weeks before my twelfth birthday, when Poppa planted watermelon seeds in our backyard. He watered the seeds faithfully, weeded the plants diligently and waited patiently for them to grow into huge, oblong watermelon like we saw in the grocery store. And the melons did grow. But then they stopped. For some unknown reason the melons stopped growing and just hung on the vines, green and round and small, not at all like what we had expected.

"Poppa," I groused, "something's wrong. Those melons are not turning out the way they're *supposed* to."

But Poppa kept watering and weeding and waiting until one day, more out of confusion and curiosity than anything else, he took a knife, chopped one of the melons off the vine and brought it into the house. I stood by the table as he whacked into the fruit and ate a piece. Then he shook his head and sighed.

Dos hoben mir nisht g'ler'nt in cheder, he whispered. "Come. Come taste. It's not at all what I expected. But it's very good." And he was right.

Later that summer I found the empty seed packet, crumpled and faded, half buried under one of the vines. The picture was faint but still clear. Poppa had planted dwarf watermelon.

To this day I don't know if Poppa planted those seeds by mistake or on purpose, to teach me a lesson. Either way, the episode had a lasting effect.

When my expectations don't bear the fruit I'd counted on, I think of Poppa's watermelon and remind myself that in life we often plant one thing and harvest something else. Something less than we hoped for. Something much different than we expected. But if we cut through our confusion and disappointment, our sadness and anger, we will find within our harvest much that is sweet.

And very good.

JUST AS A ROBIN heralds the coming of spring, Poppa's *tallis* — newly washed, flapping on the clothesline — announced the coming of Rosh Hashanah. Standing in the yard, Momma would give the *tallis* a final once-over to make sure she'd washed out each stain accumulated during the past year. Satisfied with the job she'd say, "Now. If only getting the *shmutz* out of our lives was this easy."

The run-up to the Jewish New Year offers us a chance to do significant spiritual housecleaning. We're told to examine our souls, take stock of our deeds, and review the way we've lived our lives in the past year. If we're willing to take a hard look at our dirty laundry and toss it out, we're then given a clean start and the opportunity to head in the right direction.

And so, spurred on by good intentions (or, it could be argued, by fear that doom is nigh) we spend the weeks before the New Year's arrival trying to settle past wrongs, repair family feuds, bury hatchets. On Rosh Hashanah and Yom Kippur we rush to our Synagogues and Temples, beat our breasts, repent and ask forgiveness. We promise to practice *teshuvah,* to return to the right path, in hopes that we will be inscribed in the Book of Life for another year.

Yet, when we're lucky enough to be granted more time, it's ironic how much of this precious gift we waste by procrastinating. We delay our *teshuvah* until later. Our resolutions gather dust. We put off saying *I'm sorry* or *I love you* or *thank you*. And often, by the time we do get around to saying those things, it's too late.

My Poppa understood the perils of procrastination. Like the Hebrews who made haste out of Egypt, Poppa fled the shtetl in a shot. This ability to turn on a dime served him often and well, but never better than on a long ago car trip.

Early one summer morning, Poppa, Momma, my little brother, Michael, and I, piled into our white Pontiac and headed out of Omaha toward a family reunion in Minneapolis. Poppa was at the wheel, Momma sat beside him, and Michael and I were in the back with a cooler of deviled eggs, a bundle of Batman comics and *The Good Earth*, my book of choice at the time. As we pulled out of our garage it began to rain, and the windshield wipers' rhythmic *swish swoosh, swish swoosh*, matched the measured tempo of Poppa's driving as he maneuvered the neighborhood streets and steered the Pontiac through downtown, over the Missouri River bridge and onto the Interstate.

Swish swoosh, swish swoosh. Cows, silos, rows of corn slipped by, the miles and hours, too. Hypnotized in my corner, I crawled deeper and deeper into *The Good Earth* where Wang Lung and O-lan, side by side, now plowed midwestern fields, their red paper-dressed gods recognizable in every Iowa scarecrow. *Swish swoosh, swish swoosh.* The road continued past barns (no, they were Buddhist temples) and chicken coops where hens laid deviled eggs. We drove for pages through famine, locust and the Chinese Revolution until Michael, yawning, bored with Batman, squinted out the rain-streaked window and asked, "Does everybody go through Missouri on their way from Omaha to Minneapolis?"

Momma, in a panic, screamed, "*Oi, Gottenyu.* We're going the wrong way! We must have taken a wrong turn in Des Moines. So, Alex, when we come to the next exit you'll get off and turn around."

But that form of *teshuvah* wasn't Poppa's style. Instead, right there on the Interstate, Poppa shifted gears, lurched over the median and headed back in the right direction.

Into the wide-eyed silence, Poppa explained his actions, calmly and with logic.

"Where is it written that you have to wait for an exit to turn around? The exit could be very far away. It could take a long time to get there. And furthermore, how would you feel if — when you finally did arrive at the exit — it was closed."

STILL STANDING

ACCORDING TO LEGEND, God finishes the work of Creation and decides to spend the rest of His time arranging *shidachs*—determining which baby girl will grow up to marry which baby boy. He does not, however, guarantee positive results or sign on as a Wedding Planner, for even though God (as they say) is in the details, He left the choice of rings, attendants, menu, etc., and of staying together or not, to the bride and groom.

But one item on the pre-wedding agenda would surely benefit from divine intervention. You guessed it. The Guest List. When faced with decisions re: Who & How Many, couples are often pushed to the brink.

On a balmy June evening in 1954 (far enough away from our August wedding date to allow time to print invitations and mail them) my *beshert* (Don) and I sat down with our parents to draw up the guest list.

At the time, my father was one of the rabbis at our synagogue and Don's father (Nate) was president of the congregation. Both men were well known in the community, as was my mother (Belle, the *Rebbitzen*) and Don's mother (Ruth, the First Lady, so to speak). They had special friends, of course, but because of their official positions in the congregation, both couples tried hard to be impartial and not step on toes. In other words, they understood political correctness long before it became part of the public consciousness.

So there we were, the Katz and Nogg families, sitting at the kitchen table in my folks' house. Momma laid out a tray of mandel bread and a pot of tea. Also a bottle of fancy Scotch that Poppa had received in payment for performing a *bris*. The pencils were sharp, the note pad ready. Ruth was elected recording secretary.

We began with the names of our absolutely can't-be-left-out relatives and friends. Ruth tallied up the numbers and (*yippee!*) the total was well within the quota.

We toasted one another with shots of Scotch and moving on, added our B-lists of lesser-loved aunts, uncles and cousins, plus business associates, Mah Jongg buddies and steam room cronies. Then (what the heck) we tossed in casual acquaintances who made the cut for reasons of reciprocity. Again, Ruth did the math. Again (*yahoo!*) we were shy of the quota.

"So," Momma said. "We can add more names?"

"You bet," said Poppa. "Add Gendler, Estrada, Kavich, Fogel, Perlman, Simon, Rosenberg, Yager, Roffman and Fellman. Without them I'd never have a *minyan*."

"In that case," countered Nate, "add Blacker, Venger, Rice, Kulakofsky, Rimmerman, Kaslow and Cohn. All loyal board members. Without them I'd never get a vote passed." Ruth wrote. Don poured himself another Scotch.

"Fine," said Poppa. "Fine. Then we must also add the entire staff here at *shul*, plus the *Rabbonim*, *Hazzonim*, teachers and staff from the other congregations in town. *Derech eretz*, after all, is important."

"Paramount," said Nate. "Absolutely paramount. So add the Federation Board, the ADL office and what's-his-name who weeds the cemetery."

"We should also include the Sisterhood and Men's Club," said Momma.

"With their spouses, naturally," said Ruth as she wrote.

"Naturally," said Poppa. "Also the *Chevreh Kadishah.*"

"And B'nai B'rith," said Nate. The evening was beginning to resemble a debate between the schools of Hillel and Shammai. Don tossed back another Scotch.

"Add Pioneer Women!"

"Hadassah!"

"The *Vaad haKashrut!*" The list was nearing the Fire Department's legal limit for Synagogue occupancy. Don was nearing the legal limit for alcohol consumption.

"*Mizrachi!*"

"Council!"

"*Bikur Cholim!*"

"ORT."

"And the woman who runs the *mikveh!*"

With that, my Donald lurched to his feet. "Heerz an idea, folks," he said. "Heerz an idea. You wanna make sure no one in the world feels left out, right? You wanna make sure no one falls through the cracks, right? Well, let's put an ad in the Jewish Press, okay? Let's just put an ad in the Press and invite every single person in the entire community to the wedding, okay? How's that fer an idea, folks? Waddaya think a-that?"

Ruth and Nate stared at the ceiling. My mother, envisioning the catering bill, sighed. And Poppa? He looked at Don with newfound admiration and said, "Brilliant! This solution is brilliant! My daughter is marrying a genius, a *chacham*, for sure!"

Don's totally facetious idea was actually accepted. So he killed off the rest of the Scotch.

On Sunday, August 22, 1954, at two-o'clock in the afternoon, a crowd that rivaled Yom Kippur

Day attendance filled the synagogue pews. After Don stomped on the glass, the wedding party made straight for the Social Hall, the thundering horde close behind us, tossing candy, shouting *Mazel Tov*, bloodthirsty, lusting for lox and champagne.

The first photo taken of the receiving line shows Don and me hugging my Aunt Sophie. The clock on the wall directly behind us reads 2:30, and the line of well-wishers stretches behind Sophie and out of the frame.

In another shot (3:15 exactly), Don's old fraternity brothers are pumping his hand, slapping him on the back. The line of well-wishers stretches behind the ZBT boys and out of the frame.

In yet another picture (4:27), I'm clasped to the barrel chest of a man in a Panama hat that (to this day) none of us can identify. The line of well-wishers stretches behind the stranger, etc. etc. etc.

The picture snapped at 5:03 shows Don and Bubbie in a bear hug while a pregnant woman encouragingly pats my tummy. At 5:37 (bride in stocking feet, groom with tie undone) the *shul* custodian offers his congratulations. From 6:12 to 6:39, residents of the Dr. Philip Sher Home for the Aged pinch our cheeks. And still the line of well-wishers, well... you get the picture.

Five hours after we exchanged rings, the last receiving line shot (circa 7:38) captures a tall, thin man in a long black coat, with curly red beard and *payes*. He's clutching Don's hand and whispering in his ear. Later Don told me it sounded like, "Listen good, *boychik*, and remember. *He who gives, lives.*"

By 7:45 the photographer had packed his gear and left, without so much as one picture of me in my going-away outfit. But trust me. In that periwinkle crepe suit (with peplum) and pink velvet hat (huge, like a platter) I was stunning. Like Audrey Hepburn in Sabrina.

I'm a sucker for fairy tales. A woman happy to embrace a *midrash*, suspend disbelief and say, *Yes! God the Matchmaker brought me this guy. The only one in the universe willing to stand by my side in a receiving line for over five hours.* But the rest of the marriage story? Incredible.

With no extended warranty from above, how have we survived blown gaskets, short fuses, near misses. Engine failures and breakdowns. Bad shocks. How have Don and I continued to stand and lie side by side (and now lean side by side) for fifty years?

With *mazel*. And also with Scotch.

ON A JANUARY MORNING in 1910, in the village of Vilkomir, Lithuania, my father became a Bar Mitzvah. From what Poppa eventually told me, the occasion was clearly a bare-bones event.

"It was the month of Tevet and cold, very cold," Poppa said. "Also, snowing. On a Monday morning I went with my Zeydeh to our little *shul*. I put on my *tallis* and *tefillin*. I *davened* with the men. The *rebbe* took out the Torah and yelled,

61

Alekzander Eliyahu ben Rav Zundel ha Kohen!
So I went up, said the *b'rochos* and bim, bim, bom,
that was that. Not like here in America. There
were no gifts. And unless you consider a shot of
schnapps and a dry *kichel* a celebration, there was
no party, either."

But there was an expectation. The expectation that he would continue his studies and
become a rabbi.

"Did you want to become a rabbi, Poppa?"

"Did I want to become a rabbi? Did I want
to become a rabbi, she asks. In every generation of
the Katz family there have been *rabbonim*. In
every generation since the days of Ezra the Scribe,
from whom, you should never forget, we are
descended. Did I want to become a rabbi."

So, Poppa got his *smicha*. Then, in 1923, he
left Lithuania and came to America. He married,
had my three brothers and me, and for almost
twenty years he ministered to the Jews in small
Midwestern towns. But by the time we arrived at

Beth El Synagogue in Omaha, Nebraska, Poppa realized he was ill-suited to many of the duties required of a pulpit rabbi. Delivering sermons gave him palpitations. Asking congregants for money made his palms sweat. And from the politics of synagogue life he was developing an ulcer.

So in Omaha he concentrated on the two things that gave him the most pleasure. The two things he did best. Reading Torah and teaching Bar Mitzvah boys.

As a Torah reader Poppa was uncommonly gifted. Each *trop* was flawlessly, lovingly chanted, and his dramatic interpretation of the text gave listeners goose bumps, even if the listener had zero understanding of Hebrew, which was usually the case.

As a teacher, Poppa was a veritable Pied Piper. Though students often pretended otherwise, they came to his classes willingly. More than one generation of Bar Mitzvah hopefuls sat and faced Poppa across his dark wooden desk, and into each boy Poppa tried to instill his passion for the perfect *trop* and his reverence for the Hebrew word. Bent over their *Maftir* and *Haftarah* portions, the youngsters — trying to please him, wanting his approval — did their best, but still mangled many a *munach* in the process. And during each lesson Poppa sat, elbows on his desk, head in his hands, and said, simply, *"Again."* His endurance was legendary.

So was his ability to make a point by dispensing bits of arcane Judaic wisdom and Talmudic trivia at odd moments.

One morning, a few months before his eighty–third birthday, when the *minyan* regulars were unwrapping their *tefillin*, Poppa casually said, "According to the Book of Psalms, the span of a man's life is seventy years. Even King David lived only seventy years."

The *minyan* group nodded.

"Furthermore," Poppa continued, *"Pirkeh Avot* is of the same opinion. In *Pirkeh Avot*, Rabbi

Yehuda ben Tema agrees that three score and ten is a full life. So, gentlemen, I ask you. If a man lives out his seventy allotted years, can he than start counting all over again?"

By now, the *minyan* group sensed that Poppa's *d'rosheh* was heading toward a logical, though possibly unexpected, conclusion.

"Yes, my friends, I ask you. If a man lives seventy years and chooses to start counting over again — let's say, for argument's sake, he counts another thirteen years — is that something significant and worth noting? More important, how can this apply today, in our own time?"

The *minyan* men got the message and bim, bim, bom, that was that. The Beth El congregation decided it would be a fine idea to mark Poppa's eighty-third birthday with a second Bar Mitzvah. An American-style Bar Mitzvah, by golly, with a fancy reception and the gift of a Torah commissioned especially in his honor, to make up for the no-fuss Bar Mitzvah Poppa had become at thirteen. He did not object.

And so, on a cold, snowy Shabbat in Tevet, in Omaha, Nebraska, Rav Alekzander Eliyahu ben Rav Zundel ha Kohen was called to the *bimah*, and on his second Bar Mitzvah, Poppa read Torah once more, with feeling. There wasn't a dry eye in the house.

When Poppa died, peacefully, at the age of ninety-three, the *shiva* house rang with stories. And there were good-natured debates between his old Bar Mitzvah students over which one had been the most tone-deaf. The most thickheaded. The least attentive. The rowdiest. Sitting in the *shiva* house these men were, once again, adolescent boys in Poppa's *cheder*, comparing notes and keeping score.

"So, Hymie, how many times did Katz say '*Again*' when you were learning with him?"

"And how many times did Katz take a swig

from his bottle of Scotch when you were studying with him, Sammie?"

It was sweet, listening to these now middle-aged Bar Mitzvah *bochers* verbally elbowing one another to the head of the line. Each one wanting to claim the distinction of The-Worst-Bar-Mitzvah-Student-Katz-Ever-Had.

For the record, none of my brothers became rabbis. And even though Poppa hoped I would carry on the family tradition, even indirectly, by marrying a rabbi, I did not. Surely this must have pained him. Yet even now, so many years after his death, his old Bar Mitzvah boys, his *minyan* men, his congregation, his family, still feel his influence and tell his stories.

So I ask you, Poppa. When all is said and done, is this not a legacy of which even Ezra the Scribe could be proud?

IN THE END

AS NEWLYWEDS, POPPA and Momma make a pact. He'll die first since he is, after all, fifteen years older. But it doesn't work out that way.

In her sixty-fifth year, with little warning, Momma reneges on her part of the bargain. Poppa agrees to come live with me.

"I'll be dead in a month," he says. "You'll see. Without her I won't last a month. Six weeks, tops. I'll be out of your hair in no time."

Six weeks, six months, ten months later, Poppa is still in fine fettle. Strong as an ox. Sleeping on the pullout couch in my den, fully dressed with his hat on.

"I need to be ready," he explains.

On Momma's one-year *yarzheit*, Poppa knocks back his breakfast shot of Wild Turkey, mutters, "Where is he, the delinquent?" and starts hunting for the Angel of Death.

He takes long baths, hoping to doze off and slip beneath the water. On solo walks he crosses busy streets against the light, inviting cars and taxis and bikers and buses to flatten him. He takes off his glasses and climbs up and down the basement stairs in the dark, not holding onto the rail. No luck.

"In death, as in life," Poppa sighs, "a man needs *mazel.*"

For twelve years this search for the *malach*

hamovehs consumes him. Going for broke, bare-foot, he trudges around my snowy backyard and gets frostbite. In the hospital, Poppa sees the oxygen tanks, the EKG machines, the tubes dripping medicine and says, "This is more like it."

The nurse coos, "Don't worry. We'll take good care of you." Poppa pats her hand and whispers, "Sweetheart, don't do me any favors."

Next morning, Poppa is sitting on the edge of the hospital bed, fully dressed, with his hat on.

"Listen," he says. "Last night eight patients died, but twenty three babies were born. I need a place with better demographics."

"How about we go straight to the cemetery, Pa."

"Don't get smart with your father. First I'll stop at the Beth Shalom Old People's Home."

I'm walking with Poppa in the Beth Shalom

halls when he tells me he has conversations with the Angel of Death.

"When did this start?"

"We've been on speaking terms for years," he says. "Since the day my Bubbeh died. I was four, maybe five, and he was sitting there in our house in the village, in a chair by her bed."

"So, does he really have black wings and thousands of eyes all over his body and a sword dripping poison?"

"Feh! *Bubbeh mysehs*. If you saw a man in the road with black wings and thousands of eyes all over his body and a sword dripping poison you'd run in the other direction, right? You wouldn't stop to have a chat, right?"

"Right."

"Well, the Angel of Death is no fool. He looks and dresses just like a regular person so he shouldn't scare away business. At Bubbeh's he was wearing a gabardine suit with a vest and gold watch fob. And he was smoking a cigar."

"That sounds like Dr. Feingold, Poppa."

"I went right up to him — I was a real *chutzpahdik* child — and said, 'So you're the big shot Angel of Death,' and he said, 'That's me. I don't mean to be rude, but I have another appointment, so please excuse me. See you later.' And then he climbed out the window and left. This was not Dr. Feingold. Doctors don't climb out of windows."

"They also rarely say please or excuse me."

"More proof! It was without question the Angel of Death. And he's getting closer, finally."

"Did I ever tell you about Boruch Zvi?" Poppa asks one afternoon when we're having tea in the solarium.

"Who?"

"Boruch Zvi, the crazy baker in our village. The one with the limp. I never told you about him?"

"No."

"Boruch Zvi was one of those people who thought he could outwit the Angel of Death. But whatever a person does, it's no use. You can change your name. Move out of town in the dark of night. Drink the blood of a chicken. All useless. Whatever you do, the Angel of Death will find you. Just like he found Boruch Zvi."

"He actually drank the blood of a chicken?"

"Still, Boruch Zvi's scheme was so bold, so unusual, everyone was certain it would work. What Boruch Zvi did was cover his head with a flowered shawl, pluck out every single whisker from his face — imagine the pain! — and then he started wearing his sister's clothes. Coats. Dresses. Shoes. All over the village he traipsed, wearing his sister's clothes. He looked beautiful."

"You're making this up, Poppa."

"So beautiful, in fact, that a widowed shop-keeper from Smolensk fell wildly in love with him. But cunning though the plot was, one Friday on his way to the bath-house, Boruch Zvi slipped on the ice, cracked his skull and died on the spot."

"What did he expect? With a limp and wearing his sister's shoes."

"Bingo! You have caught the irony. Not only did the Angel of Death see right through Boruch Zvi's disguise, he used it against him."

Poppa had never used the word *bingo* before.

"Wednesday is Game Night," he says.

I'm helping Poppa eat his oatmeal.

"Did I ever tell you about the time I saw the Angel of Death on the boat?" he asks.

"What boat?"

"The boat that brought me to America. What other boat."

"Was he wearing his gabardine suit with the vest and the gold watch fob and smoking a cigar like at your Bubbeh's?"

"Don't you remember what I told you? Wherever he goes, the Angel of Death dresses like everybody else, and on that boat no one was wearing a gabardine suit. No. The Angel of Death looked like a regular refugee. Rumpled clothes. Stains on his shirtfront. And he was leaning over the side throwing up. Just like the rest of us."

"Nice touch."

"On that trip he erased fifty-three names including all six Sokolof sisters. Redheads, busty. Me, he left standing."

"Timing is everything, Poppa."

"Also location, location, location."

Poppa leaves *challah* crumbs in a trail to his room, pulls the sheet over his head and holds his breath. When medicine is doled out, he swallows the water, pinches the nurse as she leaves, then hops to the toilet, spits out the pills and flushes. He stops going to meals.

Still no dice. For a man so hell bent on dying to be ignored by the Angel of Death is inexplicable.

"Maybe I'm not in his Rolodex."

"The Grim Reaper has a Rolodex?"

"What, grim. He's got a good sense of humor."

I open the door to Poppa's room and the Angel of Death, big as life, is sitting in a chair by the bed. Wings, eyes, sword, the whole nine yards.

"So, Poppa. Why isn't he dressed like a regular person. An old woman, maybe. With a walker."

The angel stretches his wings and whispers in Poppa's ear. Poppa points a finger at me.

"He says this get-up is special for you. Because you love *bubbeh mysehs.*"

"How about some water, Pa."

Again the angel whispers. Poppa nods.

"He'll pass on the water. However, he says he

would kill for a nice piece of herring. Who knew."

When I get back with the jar of fish, the Angel of Death is buttoning Poppa's coat, adjusting his hat. I hand over the herring and give Poppa a kiss on the forehead. Then he follows the angel out the window and is gone.

WHEN MY FATHER died, I inherited his books as part of the tangible legacy a rabbi leaves his child. Worn volumes of the Talmud with carefully mended spines. Dog-eared *siddurim*. A Russian *chumash*. Yiddish novels. Collections of Hebrew poetry and scholarly works on Jewish ritual and law.

But Yentl I am not.

And so it was in the more accessible English texts that I found what has become one of my favorite books, ***Worlds That Passed***. In it, the author, A.S. Sachs, describes with gentle fondness the vanished life of the *shtetl*. The hard work. The simple pleasures. The holiday celebrations that often were the only bright spots in an otherwise bleak existence.

It might be argued that *shtetl* Jews, my father included, survived from one dreary day to the next because they instinctively blocked out the reality of their cramped, poor villages and could, in Sachs' words, "soar on wings of fancy" to vast, beautiful worlds that existed only in their minds. Never were these flights more therapeutic than during *Tu B'Shevat*.

Tu B'Shevat. The New Year of the Trees. This festival that celebrates spring and the renewal of nature and life itself, always found the *shtetl* frozen and covered with snow. But no matter. On *Tu B'Shevat* the villagers transported themselves to a golden place where cedar fields, olive trees and lemon groves were heavy with buds. For a day, at least, winter was gone, and the people were in *Eretz Yisroel*, the spring sun on their backs, the land awash in milk and honey and fragrant citron. The *shtetl* Jews ate precious bits of date and almond and fig brought straight from the Holy Land! They thanked God for the fruit of the trees and prayed to stand someday inside the Gates of Jerusalem and behold with their own eyes the Cedars of Lebanon.

Actually, I don't need books to take me to this *shtetl* world. My father regularly guided me through the village where he was born and into the *cheder* where he studied from sunup to moon-rise. The *cheder* where, on *Tu B'Shevat*, lessons stopped while the *rebbe* carefully doled out raisins and nuts and *bokser*, that most exotic fruit.

According to Poppa, one *Tu B'Shevat* in the *cheder* was particularly memorable because of the aforementioned *bokser*. It seems my father's study partner, a lad named Shmuley, side-armed several pieces at another student and hit, instead, the *rebbe*. Now, a hunk of *bokser* is a mean weapon, and for Shmuley's infraction the entire class was forced to memorize an additional (and gargantuan) tractate of Talmud. Deep in my bones I'm sure that Shmuley, (if he truly existed,) was innocent and that the real culprit behind that long-ago *Tu B'Shevat Bokser Rebellion* was my Poppa.

My Poppa. How he adored trees. He told me, often and lovingly, of the trees that grew near his village. *Apple! Pear! Peach! And oh, how the fruit tasted! Much sweeter, tochter, than any fruit here in America!*

He also spoke of the weeping willow that stood by the side of his house. Its branches hung down into a pond, and under these branches, deep in the water, his mother once hid five silver spoons wrapped in a cloth. She hid them from the hooligans who periodically ransacked the village and she wound up leaving them there, in the water, when the family fled to America.

As my father grew older he lost his sight and

walked with difficulty, and his last years were like a *shtetl* winter. Dark, frightening and dismally boring. But he blocked out this reality and lived in his memory, fancifully embroidered with imagination.

He soared on wings back to the *shtetl*. It was now a thriving town.

The few trees that once grew near his village were now immense, profitable orchards that his family had owned for generations. We spoke of these riches only in private, lest the knowledge that he came from the Lithuanian landed gentry bring shame to his less fortunate contemporaries.

The treasure buried in the pond at the foot of the weeping willow grew as well. The five silver spoons multiplied into many dozens. The cache eventually included brass samovars, sterling kiddush cups and antique spice boxes encrusted with rubies and pearls. Poppa vowed to go back to the village one day. I would go with him and be his eyes, and we would find the weeping willow and the treasure in the pond which, by now, was a vast lake.

According to his doctors, my father was practicing visualization. Removing himself from pain or fear or boredom by going, in his mind, to a place of beauty, serenity and joy. But I know that Poppa was just doing what Jews have always done, when necessary. He simply blocked out the real world for a few moments and replaced it with something better. He transformed his winter into spring by returning home to his *shtetl* and to his youth, when everything was green and heavy with juicy, ripe fruit.

And so, on *Tu B'Shevat*, in the middle of my hectic life, I stop and visualize whatever brings me peace. I find a quiet world and see the olive trees. Smell the cedar and the citron. Taste the fruit. I soar on wings of fancy to secret hiding places and reclaim the treasures left there for me by my father.

THE YIZKOR SERVICE. Recited on Sukkot, Passover, Shavuot and Yom Kippur. Like a magnetic field gone haywire, it pushes us away, then pulls us in.

When I was a little girl, my Bubbie always shooed me out of *shul* before Yizkor began. "Go," she'd whisper. "You still have, thank God, a Momma and a Poppa. For you to be here isn't right. Go outside with the other children. *Go.*"

One Yom Kippur, in my rush to leave, I must pass by my playmate, Sammy Traub. *Sammy the Orphan*, some call him. Only seven, he's already a figure of mythic proportions. I squeeze around his scabby knees and feel guilt (glee?) because I have pink-cheeked parents, while Sammy does not.

Outside the synagogue, I wondered what was going on inside that we children weren't yet old enough to see or hear. "We can't be in there because they need the seats for all the dead people who come back," explained my slightly older cousin, Aaron. His reasoning made perfect, spooky sense. When I returned to my seat I looked for small clods of earth, one thread or piece of lint, some sign to prove shroud-wearing ancestors had visited. Did Sammy's mother come and hold him on her lap? Did his father smooth Sammy's hair and say, *Sha, sha, mine kaddishel. It's all right, don't cry.* The possibility gave me goose bumps. Delicious shivers.

In my teens I was still excused from Yizkor, even though by then I'd lost my Bubbie, my other grandparents and some innocence as well, and knew that dead people did not need my seat. By then I'd heard the *shtetl* old wives' tales. *Go, go, lest you arouse the jealousy of the orphan.* (Had I avoided the wrath of Sammy Traub?) *Leave, lest you say Yizkor by mistake and tempt the Evil Eye.* (Like step-on-a-crack-break-your-mother's-back, but fatal?)

By then I also knew Yizkor means *remember*. That's why my parents stayed behind. Remembering the past was their obligation, not mine, and I left them to their duty. Outside the synagogue I flirted with my current crush. Watched him puff Pall Malls (oh, how sophisticated we were!), confident no adult would find us since they were all inside (struck dumb with grief…rending their garments?) doing whatever it was that *remembering* required of them.

Soon I was a wife and mother. Even then,

before Yizkor began, I'd leave my parents in the synagogue, grab my children by the hand and flee.

When I was thirty-eight, my mother's younger sister, Betty, died. Betty, my favorite aunt. The one who wore red high-heeled pumps, smoked, told slightly raunchy jokes. The aunt who, against my mother's wishes, bought me my first lipstick when I was twelve. After Betty died, I stayed for Yizkor (how could I turn my back, *go*, not remember her?) and said the prayers with my mother. Four months later mother, too, was dead. The evil eye? A brain stem insult? Both claimed responsibility for the attack. In either case, Yizkor legitimacy was mine.

It's now thirty years that I've recited Kaddish for my mother. Ten for Poppa. Like Sammy Traub, I am an orphan, a Yizkor veteran. I know the drill.

Yizkor. May God remember the souls of my parents who have gone to their eternal home. In loving testimony to their lives I pledge charity to help perpetuate ideals important to them. Through such deeds, and through prayer and memory, are their souls bound up in the bond of life. May I prove worthy of the gift of life and the many other gifts with which they blessed me. May they rest eternally in dignity and peace. Amen.

Yizkor is a stone thrown in the moving river. The circles spread. *May God remember the souls of my mother and father and of all my relatives and friends. May God remember the souls of all the departed in this congregation. The souls of our martyrs. The six million. (Sha, sha, in chorus. It's alright, don't cry.)*

But inevitably, before the Yizkor prayers comes the parade.

Children march, tumble out the door. Their antennae pick up signals from distant galaxies, and still we try to shield them. (From what?) Grown men and women stride up the aisle. (Have they lost no one? Do their parents lie in nursing homes?) Grown men and women leave, slowed only slightly by the heavy drag of superstition, its teeth clamped to their trouser legs, their hems, like a tenacious hound. (From what do we try to shield ourselves?)

Ah, that's a question. And there are more.

Am I worthy of the gift of life and all the other blessed gifts my parents gave me? Have I passed my values to my children, as my parents did for me? Will my children gain inspiration from my life as I have from my parents' lives? Will my children do good in my name?

When they are orphans, will they remember me?

GLOSSARY

Afikomen	Hidden piece of matzah; the child who finds it during the seder wins a prize
Adir Hu	Tune sung during Passover seder
Bar Mitzvah	Ceremony initiating a Jewish boy into manhood at thirteen
Beshert	Fate; destiny
Bikur Cholim	Group that visits the sick
Bimah	Reader's stand in the synagogue
Bochers	Young men
Bokser	Carob
Bris	Ritual circumcision
B'rochos	Blessings
Bubbie	Grandmother
Bubbeh mysehs	Old wives' tales
Chacham	A wise person; a scholar

Chad Gadya	One Kid; folksong that ends Passover Haggadah
Cheder	School for Jewish boys
Chevreh Kadishah	Holy brotherhood; group that prepares bodies and buries the dead
Chometz	Leaven; not eaten on Passover
Chumash	First five books of the Hebrew Bible
Chutzpahdik	Brazen, arrogant
Davened	Prayed
Dayenu	Enough
Derech Eretz	Principles of etiquette and respect
D'rosheh	Interpretation of Torah or Talmudic text
Dreidel	Four-sided top spun on Hanukkah
Eretz Yisroel	The Land of Israel
Ganeyvim	Thieves
Gribenehs	Crisp, fried chicken skin
Gedempteh	Stewed

Gelt	Gifts of money, given at Hanukkah
Haftarah	A selection from the Prophets
Haggadah	Text that tells of the Exodus from Egypt, recited at the Passover seder
Hallel	A group of Psalms praising God
Hazzonim	Cantors
Hillel & Shammai	Ancient rabbis, known for their debates
Kaddish	Prayer for the dead
Kaddishel	Son who recites prayers of remembrance for a dead parent
Kichel	A simple cookie
Latkes	Crisp fried potato pancakes
Maccabees	Heroes of the Hanukkah story
Maftir	The concluding reading from the Torah on Shabbat and festivals
Malach Hamovehs	Angel of Death
Maoz Tzur	Rock of Ages; Hanukkah hymn

Mazel	Luck
Midrash	Interpretation of biblical text; lessons taught through stories and folktales
Mikveh	Ritual bath
Minyan	Quorum of ten adults necessary to recite certain prayers
Mizrachi	A Zionist organization
Munach	A musical note (see trop)
Peretz, Y.L.	Jewish writer (1852-1915)
Pesach	Passover; festival commemorating the Exodus from Egypt
P'cha	Aspic made from calf's feet
Pirkeh Avot	*Sayings of Our Fathers*; collection of rabbinic sayings and proverbs
P'tui p'tui	Superstitious spitting over the shoulder to keep away the evil eye
Purim	Festival celebrating the story of the Book of Esther
Rebbe, Rabbonim	Rabbi(s)
Rebbitzen	Rabbi's wife

Rosh Hashanah	Jewish New Year
Seder	The ceremony and meal that takes place on the first two nights of Passover
Sholom Aleichem	Pen name of Sholem Rabinovitch (1859-1916) Yiddish author
Shiva	The seven days of mourning following the burial
Shmutz	Dirt
Shochet	Ritual slaughterer of animals for kosher food
Shtetl	Small Eastern European village
Shul	Synagogue
Siddurim	Prayer books
Smicha	Rabbinical ordination
Tallis (tallit)	Prayer shawl
Talmud	Commentaries on Torah and Oral Law
Talmud Torah	Hebrew school
Tefillin	Phylacteries
Teshuvah	Repentence; return

Tochter	Daughter
Torah	First five books of the Hebrew Bible
Traif	Non-kosher
Trop	Musical notes used when chanting Torah portions and Haftarah
Tsimmis	A mixture of carrots, prunes and meat
Vaad haKashrut	Group that sanctions food to be Kosher
Yarzheit	Anniversary of a person's death
Yizkor	Memorial service for the dead
Yom Kippur	Day of Atonement; holiest day of the Jewish year
Zeydeh	Grandfather
Zuzim	Middle eastern coins